YOURS TRULY

AN ATONED SINNER

Lewis Wamwanda

THE WRITER'S PEN PUBLISHERS

First Edition: March 2020

Published by The Writer's Pen Publishers

(www.thewriterspen.co.ke)

ISBN: 978-1-71613-740-2

Note for Librarians:

A cataloguing record for this book is available from Kenya National Library Services

Dedication

To My Mother, Elizabeth Immo, for teaching me about forgiveness and the need to do good.

Acknowledgements

I thank everyone who encouraged me to write, my family for being there for help. I thank Esther Andaye for her editorial support and encouragement. Special thanks to Ruth Jemjor, for her believe in me. I thank Webstar Ochora for being a friend indeed, his support is enough. Finally, to Dr. Imali Abala for her support and advice, her book, *The Dreamer,* motivated me to write this book.

I won't forget to mention Hellen Kironji, A friend who is always there to listen to my fantasies and dreams and still believe in me

Dear Reader,

I write this letter to atone for my sins, as I rot in this dark dungeon, I hope no one will follow me here, I urge you to repent and ask for forgiveness to whoever you wronged before it's too late, Remember to always do the right thing. No regrets.

Yours Truly.

Table of Contents

Letter to Solomon

A Friend

Former Workmate

Former Inmate

To Solomon Makavi, a friend, workmate and former inmate.

If I could Bring Back Time, then I could Make things right for both of us, for four years I never spoke of my ordeals, but I feel like I owe you an explanation.

I still write to you this long letter, Find time to read it and forgive my deeds.

Dear Solomon,

I heard that you are leaving tomorrow,

I am in confinement, and I doubt if I'll see you leave

Risking is bad they say

But worth it if it is important, I say

I'm not allowed to put thoughts on paper

Not allowed to let my pen bleed

A crime they say, treason to the nation

Still, I risk

Now, enough of the wordings

I have a message for you

As you take your leave

Don't forget to pass it through

I have a letter for James

A letter for Peninah, my wife

I have a message for Megan, my son

Another one for Malcolm, my bastard son

For four years you've been my friend

Advised me against feuds

Did you not lend me your shirt?

I ask for another favor still

My wife is missing me I know,

She waits by the gate every dawn

Hopes for my return every dusk

Don't tell her, not yet.

My son is almost a man

That I'm sure of

Send my greetings to him

Don't mention of hopes and faith

This dungeon smells of rot

Big rats hover around in the dark

I strain to write

My hands ache still

Either way, I hope my message will be clear

Clear enough for Peninah to understand

For Megan to read out loud

I hope Natalia is beautiful like her mother

If the guards ask why you got a paper

Just incase you are caught in this muddle

Face him like a wounded lion

The way I always do many times

Tell him of the President's wish

Of a letter delivered to him

Or better still read out loud

My son will be a president too.

I have a lot to write,

Many things need to be said

Give me a little more time

My hands cant hold for long

Yesterday I fought with a guard

It wasn't fair for him to treat John like that

Just because John has no right hand

I noticed he lucks a toe on his right foot

But that isn't important now

Just explaining why I'm in confinement

The reason why my hand aches

My eyes are sore too

You wonder why I never told you everything

Doubted of my loyalty to you,

But I kept that secret you shared

Of how you killed the minister's daughter

Solomon,

Take a risk for once

Don’t be silenced by the pigs' mouth

A pig’s mouth is for the dirt

Forgive me if I write more,

I have no one to talk to,

Even the guards distaste me

In you alone I confide.

Now that you are leaving

I hope not to see you back

“Ouch” my back aches

Lay your head low

I have some confessions for you,

I have a word to share

Solomon.

I will remember the four years we shared.

You still wonder why I kept silent

I atone for my sins

Smaller sins to count

Silence serves better

You killed the Minister's daughter

So you think , dear best friend

I watched her die

You slept on the floor, drank

Your honesty was too loud

Shook the walls of the high

Like Judas of the bible

I was bought to set you up

The system is rotten

So is me,

I atone for my sins

I killed her, the Minister's daughter.

Solomon.

Money is the root to all evil

You have to understand, I have a family

My children needed food too

Though for four years you stayed here,

Thinking of how evil you were

Guilt and shame to soothe you

Now I wash you hands clean

I stabbed your back, I know

But don't stab back

The Good Book talks of forgiveness

Seventy times or so

I was a true friend

And still I am,

But the Pigs threatened

Like a slave I had to obey

Now look at me,

In a dark dungeon

Like a caged bird ready for sale

Or a slave ready for execution

A thousand ways to say sorry

Yet I paint this paper with ink

I can offer words

Silver and gold I have none

So when you leave for home

Pass by my dungeon

Take these letters with you

I know of the wages of sin

I free your mind with the truth

Offload your burden of guilt

Go home in peace

Don’t live here a piece

Wait a second,

I can't hide the joy anymore

These drafted letters will be sent

You will be my messenger I hope

Pass by Obadiah's house

On your way to my wife's

Don't tell her of my where about

It's a shame, isn't it?

Tell Obadiah to marry my wife

Tell him to school my sons

A small favor for an old friend

Plead with him.

My wife's bed is cold

And someone needs to warm it

But until I leave this dungeon

Ask Obadiah for help

I won't regret if she bears him a daughter

Or better still get him more sons

Let them get married in a church

The church bell will reach my ears

My wife is good in bed

Caring and knows how to play

She isn't a screamer though

I know this will please him

As you take your leave

Tell Obadiah to marry my wife

To share a bed with her

Till I get out of this dungeon

Letter to Peninah

My Wife and Mother to My Children

To Peninah Saumu, You will forever be the mother to my children.

I know it's long since I came home, but I will come, no doubt.

I felt like I owe you an explanation, and as I write this long letter, I hope you will understand and forgive me my transgressions.

I love you Mama Meghan.

Dear wife,

I don't know where to start from,

Forgive my manners,

I should have started with a greeting

I have lost my manners

Hello dear wife

Mother to Meghan Makori

I heard I got a daughter too

Natalia Makori.

I hope you are fine

I have faith of that for sure

I won't lie to you dear Peninah

Fleas and ticks feast on my flesh daily

I am just kidding, smiles

I am on an errand my dear

Working for the nation, for the good of the citizens

Peaceful and patriotic ones

I will come home, for sure I know

Carried with energetic men

Like a King, only that I'll be sleeping

But that is not important for now

I have a lot of stories to tell

I hope you have a lot of time to read

I lost count of days,

Months and years unknown

You got questions to ask

I believe this letter will answer them all

Dear wife, dear Peninah

Don’t shed a tear when you read this

Six years ago, I left for work

Never did I mention about my work

You had all the reasons to doubt me

I did it all to protect my family

How could I tell you about me,

That Like chicken, I slaughter men

Men who went against the high

The bigger pigs I mean

I am the holder of truth

I help 'em play dirty games

Forgive me Peninah

I was the one who killed your brother

I had to, Sacrifice.

His life for my family's

Tell me, could I let you die

Watch a fountain of blood from your throat?

Your father didn't die of accident too

Your mama saw me kill him

I had to protect my secret

I atone for my trespasses

I am symbol of a black nation

Like a bird of prey, I kill to survive

I loved you not, I'm sorry

You were a passage to your father's chambers

He had all charges against me

He had evidence against the pigs

All the pens the pigs occupied

Their lavish and posh houses

I helped the pigs steal land

Even the house you live in, our house

Stolen from Mama Baraka

The old lady who sells rotten fish

Now listen,

I atone for my sins, I live in a dungeon

Kept away from light and the world

I will die of guilt

My hands are red as beetroot

Blood drop drip to my feet

I hear them scream for help

Begging for their lifeless life

I laughed watching them die

I laughed when I went through their wives

Pleasure and pain, nobody cared

Forgive me

Your life is in danger too

The pigs doubt you know of my secrets

Like a good wife to her husband

Poor you.

They will send men in boots

Pose like men in blue

Torture you with words

Be strong, like the man you married

I killed the Minister's daughter

Set up Solomon for the murder

For four years he's been in

Innocently paying for deeds undone

A month later I was brought in

That I posed a threat to the nation

And the good citizens of the country

Rotten system.

The pigs dine and wine

Laugh for the achievements they never made

Watching their stomachs grow with dirty food

A symbol of greed

They con people of their money

Taxes are higher than normal

Taking credits too high to be paid

Squander pennies like there's no tomorrow

Dear Wife,

I know about your love for the church

The preaching from Pastor Peter

Against corruption and injustice

I killed Pastor John

Paid by Pastor Peter to complete the job

His hunger for tithes and offerings

Surpassed his love for humanity

He preaches of peace and love

Yet walk with bodyguards for security

I heard of his appointment fee

Fit to buy a goat and its kid

Religion has made us slaves

People have turned away from The Most High

They worship Pastor Peter

And Compete of the highest tither

Pastor Peter is so generous

Donates children to widowed women

And sometimes add two or three to married women

He has a wife.

You wonder why I hate churches

Pastor Peter owns four pubs in town

Two Brothels in the city

And a club in the village

That was none of my business though

I left home six years ago

Yet I'm glad you got a daughter for me,

Is she three or four years old? I remember not

I have other confessions to make

Of how I forced myself into my boss's wife

In the line of duty five years ago

She died of AIDS

She left a son baring my name

His ears hear not,

Never heard him cry or talk

He doesn’t even walk, he’s five

I forced myself into an old woman too

She bled to death

Muttered things I couldn’t hear

But still I never cared

Now if you get this letter

When Solomon comes home

Soon or later

Tell your heart to forgive me

If I don’t make it out

This is true I know,

I have a wish to make

To you and our children

If I die

Don't cry out loud

I'll grow as a flower

To soothe you with my fragrance

If I die

Don't be sad

I will come as a dove

To wake you up with my soft coo

If I die

Don't mourn

I will come as a gentle wind

To wipe your tears and grief

If I die

Don't break my pot

I will come as water

To quench your thirst

If I die

Sing songs of joy

Wait for my return

In this new form of life.

Letter to My Son

Meghan Makori

To Megan Makori, now you are a man, I am sorry that I left you, I don't deserve your forgiveness but I hope this letter will try to explain my deeds.

I would trade my life to have a moment with you, to erase the pain and trauma I left it with you, to prove that I am a better dad than you think.

Take care of our home, be strong. Be wise.

Dear Son,

Are you nine or ten years old?

I lost count of years and months

Weeks and days I know not

My dungeon is ways dark

Anyway, I hope you are fine

I don't have a lot of time for greetings

But to pass my message of love

And atonement of sins

I'm sorry I left

I'm sorry ten thousand times

Only that I did it out of love

Pure fatherly love.

Son,

I have lived a life so unpleasant

Not my wish to see you follow the same path

Make your own path, men do so

Your father is a thief,

Of power and money

Love and peace

A shameless idiot to be precise

Like a candle in a cave

My light is flicking out

A void full of echoes remain

My end is near

I live in a cage like an animal

Ready for slaughter or torture

Like a slave for sale

In the name of saving the nation

I want to ask you for a favor

Take care of your mother

Protect your sister

Help you Brother Malcolm

I can’t lie to you anymore

I am a dad whose son shouldn’t be proud

Did I mention of how I grabbed lands

Embezzled funds from the government?

I did all dirty works for the government

I killed weeds and parasites

Those who wanted to spoil the good names of our pigs

In the name of truth and accountability.

I was the system controller

Before the owners of the system decided

That I knew too much to bring them down

I am not a patriot

I made deals with terrorists

To attack those who opposed us

Submission is compulsory

The government makes decisions

Education is free they say

Yet I saw the pigs take their sons abroad

To private and expensive schools

Yet pay our teachers peanuts

Like a puppet I was used

When questions arose they coiled

Named me a security hazard to the nation

Sent to the dungeon, a safe place for me

I still regret of my deeds

Sacrificed my family for power

My wife for women

My son for a bastard

Son.

When you grow up to be a man

Don't fight

Do what's right.

The system is rotten

The pigs are getting hungrier and fatter

They will devour you like a prey

Quench their thirst with your wealth

Stand like a man

Education is your key to the throne

Change the system

Kill the pigs

I won't see you again

But when I'll be burning in hell

Or by mercy dining in heaven

I will be proud of you.

Meghan, my son

Daddy is sorry to leave you

Hoping to get forgiveness and acceptance

We are still one in blood.

Now that you know your father is a murderer

Become the person the Good Book describes

Love for humanity, peacemaker

Meghan.

I did all this to put food in the table

Ask your mother If I failed to send money

Those clothes you wear are from my pockets

I am still a good father

They threatened to hurt my family

That is if I never did their dirty works

They threw me in this dark dungeon

Just because My use was over

Hungry for power,

I watched them kill the minister

Accused the terrorists for his demise

Planted their own on the throne

Their hands are not as clean as people see

They have made us drink their blood

Control us like little puppets

Like a flag to wind

They will feed with you with milk and honey

To bribe you away from your pain

To blind you from the light

People will praise them for their good works

Like sheep, follow sheepishly

To the ballot yet again cast their votes

To the parasites who devour us alive

Fight them son.

They have poisoned our citizens

We live in fear of fellow neighbors

Laughing all day long together

Holding knives at night

Fear them not,

I feel the fire burning in you

Ignite it son.

Revolution starts at home.

Son, my time in this earth is depleting

As you read this letter,

I will be rotting in jail

Eating with rats and eaten by fleas

Make me proud son

I atone for my sins

Rebel anything that comes from the pig

Face them, challenge them.

To My Son

Malcolm Makori

To My son Malcolm Makori, you serve a purpose in this world.

You are abled differently, a symbol or resistance.

Son, Daddy loves you.

I write this letter to you, to atone for my sins and urge you to follow the light.

Dear Son,

I know you are a fighter

Three years in this salty world

Has thought you strength

I heard people say that

I shed tears writing this

Not of regrets

Tears of shame and guilt

I'm sorry, son.

How could I face you, and

Tell you how I forced myself into your mother

How she begged me to spare her innocence

I watched her bleed, I heard her scream

I'm not inhumane,

Thought it was a payback to my boss

For letting me fix his poop always

Like a hyena to a lion

I'm happy that you can't hear

You won't be flattered with their sweet words

I mean the pigs

They won't buy you, no, not you

You see, you are abled differently

I know you walk not

A good thing for you son

You'll never walk into their traps

Did I forget to mention that you don’t talk?

Oh yes, you won’t tell them of your plans

Plans to redeem the patriotic citizens

Like Musa of the Good Book

I leave you to Meghan,

Not that because you are my son

But because yours heart is made of steel

Strengthen him to be a Lion, like the one in Judah

There’s a fight coming

A fight of truths and ashes

Force yourself through them all

Like how I forced myself through your mother

I hear the guards complain of sickness

Expensive medicine and services

They offered you sickness they invented

Charge you expensively for the medicine

A game of power, I say

When two bulls fight in the field

Is it the grass that get hurt?

We pay for our own ignorance

A time is coming soon

Where brothers will turn into sisters

Fathers will force themselves into their daughters

A war of blood and Ashes

I trust you son

I believe you will bring peace

Change their mindset, Malcolm

You are a child of steel

Let everyone carry their cross

I see Pigs getting away with bigger crimes

Citizens rot in jail for stealing neighbor's salt

Four years of pain and torture

They dine in expensive hotels

Pay their bills with our taxes

Yet our roads are impassable

Floods wash away our farms

These people are dirty

They collect taxes from our women

Leave them with bounties

Seen nine months later

They rob farmers off their produce

In the name of exporting them for higher returns

Import cheap products from abroad

Forcing as to pay expensively for them

Business as usual

They sell us infected foods

Lowering our lifespan

Weakening our thinking abilities

Son.

Grow old, not to be like them

Do what is right

Your conscience won't judge

Don't follow their steps

They take sons of peasants

To the dirty bloody battle fields

Yet fly their sons abroad for safety

They have filled their stomachs with booze

I talk of the pigs

Booze from our mothers' pockets

And from our fathers' toils

No rains, no food

They did away with forests

To create tall buildings

In the name of boosting the economy

Poor roads, poor medicine facilities

They'll still come five years later

Other more promises to make

Disappear after winning hearts

We drank their bloods

Nothing left to do

Rise up, you are the resistance

Wash us clean from their dirty blood.

Son, my time has ended

Don't live the life I lived

Fight like a man

Sometimes we have to.

My hands are sore

My back aches

Yet I still have two canes today

I rest my case.

Letter to Joseph

The Youth Leader

Fighter of Justice

To Joseph, I've heard of your good work of fighting for your rights, I fully support you, at least that is the least I can do after ruining my life, and that of the nation.

Fight like a wounded lion, there's still hope for liberation.

Don't be bribed by honey coated words

You are steel.

Dear Joseph,

I know you've heard a lot about me

Even though we never met at all

I know you distaste my deeds

You have every right for that

My reign is over

Reign of blood and pain

Ashes and broken skulls

My dungeon's a gift

They did this to me,

Never make a deal with the devil

He'll suck nectar from you

Throw the remains is a black dungeon

I heard of your frequent strikes

Jobless youths, poor economy

Free education without jobs

Don’t play the game

Lands have been grabbed

Farms made into quarries

Homes turned into factories

Homeless, yet words are not spoken

Our leaders are bribed

Men in blue it from the silver plates

Turning their ears away from helpless cries

I urge you to fight.

Ignite the fire your father lit

Avenge his cold blood death

I pulled the trigger

Forgive me for that, it was an order

Fear no death,

Your father didn't beg for his life

Claimed of how his first son

Will finish the work he started

I hear your story, son

Don't shudder when I call you son

Every dad will be proud to call you that

You're a threat to the pigs and those they dine with

Make noise, loud noise

Let the world know you are alive

I swear nobody will dare touch you

Not when the whole world watches, chaos.

Nobody fights well like a wounded lion

Protecting it's kingdom from the prey

You got a reason to fight

Finish what your father started.

Letter to

The Religious Leaders

I don't have a particular recipient for this letter, make as many copies as possible and distribute it to all religious leaders, I know one of ten will get the message.

Let you true purpose be seen, you are the light of the world.

The Moses of today, or Joshua of the Good Book of God.

Dear sir/madam,

You may fear to interact with the likes of us

Drunk and careless idiot

A poor murderer, a rapist and thief

But still I take my chances

First, I ask for forgiveness

Persecuting one of your own

Is a sin not forgivable?

I am Saul from the book of Acts

I am beyond saving, I suppose

Out there, many rot in the darkness

Darkness you ought to light a light

Don't forsake them

I pray that you find your way
A way to stop religion from making you slaves
Do what's right in the eyes of the Most High
Truth and honesty be your guide

Find a way to replace Pastor Peter
His transgressions has made the church dirty
He has a whole church under his command
The Sunday school is filled with his blood

He preaches of love and peace on daylight
Dine with the pigs at night
In the company of women and wine
They laugh at the foolishness of believers

Run away from the dark

That threatens to engulf your alters

Darkness of greed and power

Preach the gospel instead

I may not be so religious

Once in a while I read the Good Book

And I know of How Jesus did to Saul

I would wish to be named Paul

I follow his footsteps

Writing letters to the churches ages ago

I, too, write letters of atonement to those I wronged

I am washed by the blood of Jesus

Teach your flocks to do good

Guide them on how to keep a neighbor

War is coming,

Your neighbor will be your savior

Tithes and offerings are good

But unlike Pastor Peter

Put them into use

Let's all see their benefits

I pray that you forgive me

Isn't it written in the Bible?

Don't you teach about forgiveness?

The same way Jesus did.

Pray for our system

In your daily prayers for men

The pigs are devouring us

We turn to the creator for help

You wonder why we remain silent

And can't voice our griefs

And you try to find help

Please do, we are okay not

You see us die one by one

You fear the morgue will over flood

The cemetery will vomit others

We can't complain though

You see them asking us to fight

And we raise hands on brothers

And find pleasure in our sister's chambers

We are not fine with it.

We drank their blood

And their is nothing we can do

But to let them control us

Or face their wrath and anger

We drank their blood

Their dirt infected blood

That defiles our system

To submit to their wants

I leave that to you

Letter to The Citizens

I don't know what to tell you, your letter will be short, I assume you always know what's right for the society.

Change your ways, open your eyes.

Dear Citizens,

You leave thieves in the parliament
Go ask the government
They steal billions of shillings
But when they come near you
You lick their buttocks
And encourage them to steal more

Is it fair at all? Is it?
Go to the parliament,
That is where the real thieves are, go
They still steal billions from us
Shamelessly, in the broad light
They are the real thieves.

I heard of a boy, a thief of daily bread
Not even twenty years old, not Eighteen
Poor and hungry
And there you were, full of rage and anger

Threatening to burn him

Is it fair? Now tell me, is it fair?

We are busy encouraging those that steal billions

And threaten to burn those that steal peanuts

What is wrong with you! Hypocrites!

Is it fair?

Go burn the government!

Don't call yourselves Citizens

You are weak, shameless Nation

This blood you shade won't appease anybody

Cowards! Go burn the real thieves

Take your rage to the Parliament, Stupid!

Is it fair? Tell me, have you never stolen before?

You leave the thieves live in mansions

When you share slums with Rats

Is it fair?

To burn the ones who share your fate?

Go ask the government

Go to the parliament

There is where the real thieves are.

Is it fair?

Idiots! Cowards!

Afraid to face the real thieves

And want to burn a poor hungry boy

Is it fair?

To lick their buttocks,

You cheer and encourage them to steal from you

Change your ways, do the right

Letter to The Pigs

This will be my final letter to write, I hope each letter will reach its recipient.

I know your plans, I know that tomorrow I will face the rope for the good of the patriotic citizens.

I call you Pigs because I lack suitable names to call you, anyway, a pig is a good animal, never complains about food, eats anything from anywhere.

So are you.

Dear Pigs,

I'm disappointed.

The only truth I know is the truth

The only system I know has failed

It failed my mother and father

My sisters and brothers are beyond saving

And now, it is failing me.

The system has failed us

You have failed us

The other day I watched the poor cry

While you added more to your dishes

Grabbing the leftovers now

The less fortunate trek in search of education
With soap and scrap metal for their upkeep
What did you do about it?

You all have eyes
Eyes that see the tax evaders
Eyes that see not the pockets that spill notes
You see not the bellies that devour the poor.
But still, you got eyes to see the strong win

Should I cry?

Perhaps a laugh will ease the pain
The pain of seeing the poor helping the poor
And the rich grabbing from the helpless poor folks
I repeat

You have failed us

So, where do we run when we have no food?

Do we run to our fellow poor folks?

To give them hope of a Tomorrow that never comes

To remind them that we are cursed by poverty

And soon we will rot and smell of poverty

Or do we run to the fortunate pigs

Who lay in mowed grass under the shade of their huge umbrellas

And feed their dogs with six kilos of meat each hour

Do we run to you who give your buttocks for us to lick

When we have no salt in our kitchens

We run to neighbors for a scoop or two

But how will we run to fellow neighbors

Who erect five feet barriers

To keep away the plague of poverty from them?

Neighbors who turn our sons away from us

You Pigs!

You collect taxes from our shanties

And leave our women with grown bellies

You have failed us.

Now, where are you when we call for help

Will we rely on well wishers? Will we?

Education is meant to be the key of life

What you forgot to tell us all along

Education is the key to life, yes

But to the men and women with big bellies

Should I say pigs?

And their "God-sent" piglets

Who fly above with choppers and jets

Afraid to be infected with poverty

You have failed us

We cry our griefs to deaf ears

Not forgetting to show our troubles to blind eyes

Shame! Shame on you!

You will feed us with honey and milk

To bribe us away from the pain

But the memories will be buried deep within us

Plunging deep down the thoughts of sorrow

Like a small ship lost in the middle of a raging sea

Or a plane in the middle of a stormy night

And silently, within the verge of our sorrow

We will summon death for comfort

And take pain with us

To ease the burden in our hearts

We will laugh together 'till midnight

To give you hopes of triumph

And a sense of victory and pride

But when we lay silently in our beds

In the cold lonely nights,

The buried memories will find their way out

To torment and lure us to pain

Mocking and making fun at us

As we bath in tears of our sorrows

And fighting ourselves back to slumber

Nights will not be time to sleep

For fear will be roaming at the darkest hours

Waiting to pounce on our beaten souls

And take control of the long nights

We will be enslaved by our memories

Tortured by the past bitter pains

To the point of breaking our souls

And killing the little joy we possessed

Extinguishing the light lit years ago

Hope and happiness will float in the dark

We will laugh and smile all day

And you will praise us for our happiness

And urge others to be like us

To follow the steps we ought to make

But you won't understand our griefs

And not notice the masks we wear

That fades as dusk approaches

Leaving us naked, afraid and lonely

And the chains of fear will be put on us

As we wait for our long night of torture

You won't see the sorrow behind our joy

Neither The ugly part of our beauty

Nor sense the fears behind our courage

For our masks are only worn at dawn

To give us a false impression of joy

Of courage, of happiness and of love

And you will marvel and make merry

Of how you succeeded to change us

And people will praise and sing songs for you

But we will still wait for night, for torture

These are what we pass through daily

Because of your selfish deeds

Your greed surpasses your humanity

Pigs!

Like an ox pulling a wagon

Sweating and breathing

Moaning at the load behind

are your minds, tired and wasted

You believe in making a better tomorrow

And perfecting a remaining today

Forgetting the fight of yesterday

That killed the better half of yours

You claim to be heroes,

Fought and won your freedom

But a lie it is, you fear to face

For yesterday, you fought and died

Freedom is happiness

Happiness is love

Love is for the chosen few

You, you were killed by your burdens

You watch silently,

As you kill your own remains

You cry tearlessly

For the tears were wasted yesterday

You died yesterday,

As you struggled for power

Not seen, not felt

You died yesterday.

Do something dear pigs

Or your story will end like the story I once read

"The Animals Farm"

Does it ring in your dirty minds?

Yours Truly

My clock is ticking now

My lifespan almost ending

Tomorrow I face the rope

Never to see light again

Don't end up here too

I atone for my sins

My hands are aching

My heart's at peace

Remember to be good

Nobody may watch

But your conscience does

Goodbye dear reader.

Yours Truly

A saved sinner.

www.ingramcontent.com/pod-product-compliance
Lightning Source LLC
Chambersburg PA
CBHW071707030726
47598CB00012B/2566

9781716137402